HPS 1443

STEVE REICH
PROVERB

for Voices, Vibraphone and Keyboards

HENDON MUSIC

BOOSEY & HAWKES

AN IMAGEM COMPANY

DISTRIBUTED BY

7777 W. BLUEMOUND RD. P.O. BOX 13819 MILWAUKEE, WI 53213

www.boosey.com
www.halleonard.com

Co-commissioned by the
BBC Proms as part of their 100th Anniversary season in 1995
and the
Early Music Festival of Utrecht.

First performed as a partial work in progress on September 7, 1995, Royal Albert Hall, London, by the BBC Singers with members of the Ensemble Modern, Peter Eötvös, conductor.

During the following two months the original seven minutes were thoroughly revised, and the piece was completed in December, 1995. The American premiere of the finished work was performed February 10, 1996 at Lincoln Center by The Theater of Voices and members of the Steve Reich Ensemble, Paul Hillier, conductor.

Published by Boosey & Hawkes Inc
229 West 28 St, Floor 11
New York, NY 10001

www.boosey.com

AN IMAGEM COMPANY

ISMN 979-0-051-21443-3
HPS 1443

First impression 2015

Note by the Composer

The idea for *Proverb* was originally suggested to me by the singer and conductor Paul Hillier who thought, primarily, of a piece with six voices and two percussion. What resulted was a piece for three sopranos, two tenors, two vibraphones and two electric organs, with a short text by Ludwig Wittgenstein. Since Paul Hillier is well known as a conductor and a singer of early music, and since I share an interest in this period of Western music, I looked once again at the works of Perotin (School of Notre Dame – 12th century) for guidance and inspiration.

The three sopranos sing the original melody of the text in canons that gradually augment, or get longer. The two tenors sing duets, or commentaries, in shorter rhythmic values against held tones from the sopranos. The two electric organs double the singers throughout and further fill in the harmonies. The constantly changing meter groupings of twos and threes give a rhythmically freeing quality to the voices. After about three minutes of just voices and organ, the vibraphones enter enunciating these interlocking shifting groups of twos and threes.

The original theme in the voices is then inverted, and moves from B minor to E♭ minor. In this contrasting section, the original descending melodic line becomes an ascending one. The last part of this piece is one large augmented canon for the sopranos and baritone, returning to the original key of B minor, with the tenors singing their melismatic duets continuously as the canon slowly unfolds around them. This is concluded by a short coda which ends with a single soprano.

Though the sopranos sing syllabically, one note for each word, (every word of the text is monosyllabic) the tenors sing long melismas on a single syllable. Perotin's influence may be heard most clearly in these tenor duets against the sopranos, clearly resembling three part Organum. That same influence plays a more indirect role in the soprano augmentation canons which are suggested by the held tenor notes in Perotin's Organum.

The short text, *"How small a thought it takes to fill a whole life!"* comes from a collection of Wittgenstein's writings entitled *Culture and Value.* Much of Wittgenstein's work is 'proverbial' in tone and brevity. This particular text was written in 1946. In the same paragraph from which it was taken, Wittgenstein continues, "if you want to go down deep you do not need to travel far."

–Steve Reich

Anmerkung des Komponisten

Die Idee zu meiner Komposition Proverb kam ursprünglich von Sänger und Komponist Paul Hillier. Er schlug mir vor ein Stück für sechs Stimmen und zwei Perkussionsinstrumente zu schreiben. Letzen Endes wurde daraus ein Stück für drei Soprane, zwei Tenöre, zwei Vibraphone und zwei elektrische Orgeln sowie ein kleiner Text von Ludwig Wittgenstein. Da Paul Hillier als Komponist und Sänger von Früher Musik weitläufig sehr bekannt ist und ich mich ebenso für diese Musikepoche westlicher Musik interessiere, vertiefte ich mich ein weiteres Mal in die Werke von Perotin (Notre Damer Schule, 12. Jahrhundert), die mir als Leitfaden und Anregungen dienten.

Die drei Soprane singen die originale Melodie als Kanons, die entweder stetig an Lautstärker zunimmt oder länger wird. Die zwei Sänger singen Duette oder Kommentare kürzerer rhythmischer Elemente als Kontrast zu den lang gehaltenen Tönen der Soprane. Durch die ganze Komposition hinweg doppeln die zwei elektrische Orgeln die Stimmen der Sänger und reichern zusätzlich die Harmonien an. Durch das konstante Wechseln von zwei und drei Schlagtaktarten erhalten die Stimme einen freien Charakter. Nach ca. 3 Minuten Gesang und Orgel treten die Vibraphone hinzu um diesen Taktartenwechseleffekt deutlicher zu untermalen.

Das ursprüngliche Thema der Stimmen wird invertiert und bewegt sich weg von H Moll zu Eb Dur. In diesem kontrastvollem Abschnitt werden die ursprünglich absteigenden melodischen Linien zu aufsteigenden. Der letzte Teil dieses Stückes ist ein lang ausgedehnter Kanon für Soprane und Baritone, der zur ursprünglichen Tonart H Moll zurückkehrt. Die Tenöre singen derweil kontinuierlich ihre melismatischen Duette während der Kanon sich um sie herum entfaltet. Abgeschlossen wird dieser musikalische Vorgang durch einen kleinen Coda, der durch einen einzigen Sopran abschliesst.

Obwohl die Soprane sillabisch singen, d.h. eine Note pro Wort, (jedes Wort des Textes ist monosyllabisch) singen die Tenöre lange Melismen auf einer einzigen Silbe. Der Einfluss Perotins mag wahrscheinlich am meisten während den Tenorduetten zur Geltung kommen, die sich sehr dem dreisätzigen Organum ähneln. Derselbe Einfluss spielt in den Soprano lauterwerdenden Kanons eine eher indirekte Rolle, der durch die gehaltenen Tenornoten auch in Perotins Organum angewandt wurde.

Der kurze Text *"How small a thought it takes to fill a whole life!"* stammt aus einem Schreiben Wittgensteins namens *Culture and Value*. Vieles von Wittgensteins Arbeiten ist sprichwörtlich kurz und bündig toniert. Dieser Text wurde 1946 geschrieben. Aus selbigen Paragraph stammt auch Wittgensteins "if you want to go down deep, you do not need to travel far".

—Steve Reich

Note du compositeur

L'idée à l'origine de *Proverb* me fut suggérée par le chanteur et chef d'orchestre Paul Hillier qui pensa, en premier lieu, à une pièce à six voix et deux percussions. Il en résulta une pièce pour trois sopranos, deux ténors, deux vibraphones et deux orgues électriques sur un bref texte de Ludwig Wittgenstein. L'intérêt que je partage avec Paul Hillier, réputé pour son expertise dans le domaine de la musique ancienne, pour cette période de la musique occidentale, me conduisit à me tourner de nouveau vers les œuvres de Pérotin (École de Notre-Dame – XIIème siècle) en quête de références et d'inspiration.

Les trois sopranos présentent la mélodie initiale portant le texte en canons en augmentation rythmique progressive ou de durée graduellement allongée. Les deux ténors chantent des duos, ou commentaires, en valeurs rythmiques plus brèves sur les notes tenues des sopranos. Les deux orgues électriques doublent continuellement les chanteurs et complètent les harmonies. Les changements constants de regroupements rythmiques par deux ou par trois confèrent un contour libre aux voix. Après environ trois minutes occupées par les seuls voix et orgues, les vibraphones font leur entrée en énonçant ces configurations par deux ou par trois entremêlées et fluctuantes.

Le thème original présenté par les voix est alors inversé et se déplace de *si* mineur à *mi* bémol mineur. Dans cette section contrastée, la ligne descendante liminaire se transforme en ligne ascendante. La dernière partie de la pièce consiste en un large canon en augmentation entre sopranos et baryton revenant à la tonalité première de *si* mineur, les ténors chantant leurs duos mélismatiques sans interruption tandis que le canon se déroule lentement autour d'eux. L'œuvre se conclut par une courte *coda* achevée par un seul soprano.

Tandis que les parties des sopranos sont syllabiques, figurant un mot par note (chaque mot du texte étant monosyllabique), les ténors développent de longs mélismes sur une seule syllabe. L'influence de Pérotin est la plus marquée dans la simultanéité des duos de ténors et des lignes des sopranos qui rappelle l'*organum* à trois voix. Cette même influence joue un rôle plus indirect dans les canons des sopranos en augmentation, inspirés des notes tenues de ténor dans l'*organum* de Pérotin.

Le texte bref, *"How small a thought it takes to fill a whole life"* (*"Comme il suffit d'une infime pensée pour remplir toute une vie'*) est extrait d'une recueil d'écrits de Wittgenstein intitulé *Culture et valeur*. Une grande partie de l'œuvre de Wittenstein se révèle « proverbiale » par son ton et sa concision. Dans le même paragraphe de ce texte datant de 1946, Wittgenstein poursuit : « Si l'on désire creuser en profondeur, il n'est nul besoin de voyager loin. »

–Steve Reich

Performance Notes

<u>Instrumentation</u>

3 Lyric Soprano singers

2 Tenor singers

2 Vibraphones (motor off throughout)

4 Keyboards
(2 players playing 4 five-octave electric keyboards)

Duration: *ca.* 14 minutes

<u>Stage Setup</u>

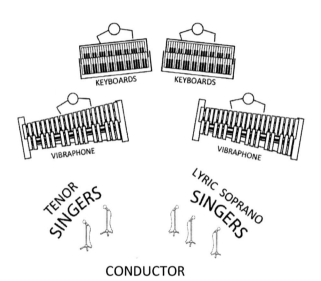

CONDUCTOR

All singers sing non-vibrato throughout. A background of singing Medieval and Renaissance music will usually be helpful. Familiarity singing with a microphone is also desirable.

The sound in both samplers is a Baroque Organ sample that is available from Boosey & Hawkes. If this sample is not available, a non-vibrato mild double reed sound is usually available on most synthesizers or electric organs. In any event, four keyboards are necessary.

•

Alle Sänger singen ohne Vibrato. Erfahrung im Singen von Mittelalterlicher und Renaissance Musik ist von Vorteil. Vertrauter Umgang mit mikrofoniertem Singen ist wünschenswert.

Der Sound in beiden Samplern ist eine Barockorgel, die bei Boosey&Hawkes erhältlich ist. Sollte dieses Sample nicht erhältlich sein, sollte ein nicht vibrato weicher doppelrohrblattinstrumentenähnlicher Sound, wie sie auf den meisten Synthesizern oder elektrischen Orgeln vorhanden sind, gewählt werden. Vier Keyboarder sind absolut notwendig.

•

Tous les chanteurs chantent non-vibrato partout. Un fond de chants de la musique médiévale et de la Renaissance seront généralement utiles. Familiarité chante avec un micro également souhaitable.
Le son dans les deux échantillonneurs est un échantillon d'orgue baroque qui est disponible chez Boosey & Hawkes. Si cet échantillon ne sont pas disponibles, une double son doux non-vibrato roseau est généralement disponible sur la plupart des synthétiseurs ou des organes électriques. Dans tous les cas, quatre claviers sont nécessaires.

• Performance materials are available from the Boosey & Hawkes Rental Library •

for Paul Hillier

P R O V E R B

STEVE REICH
(1995)

Soprano 1: How small a thought it takes to fill a whole life!

Sop. 1: How small a thought How small a thought it takes to fill a

Sop. 2: How small a thought it takes to fill

979-0-051-21443-3

Text from CULTURE AND VALUE by Ludwig Wittgenstein
Copyright © 1977 Used by permission of Blackwell Publishers
and University of Chicago Press, publishers.

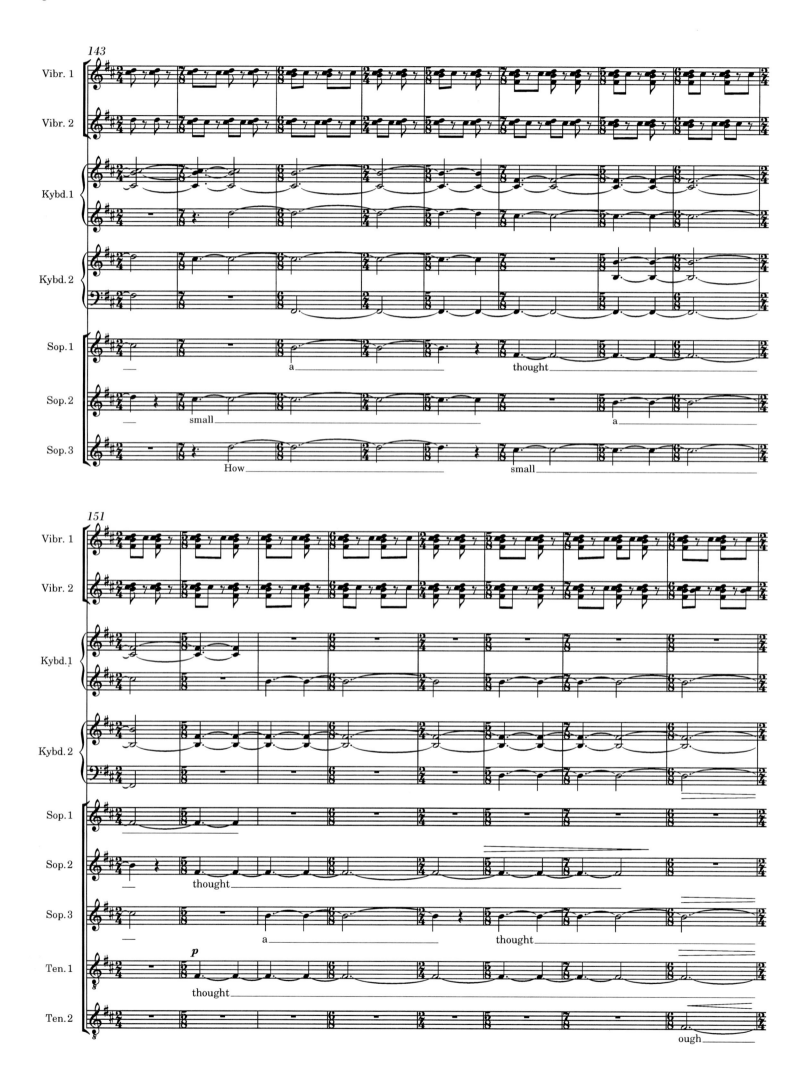

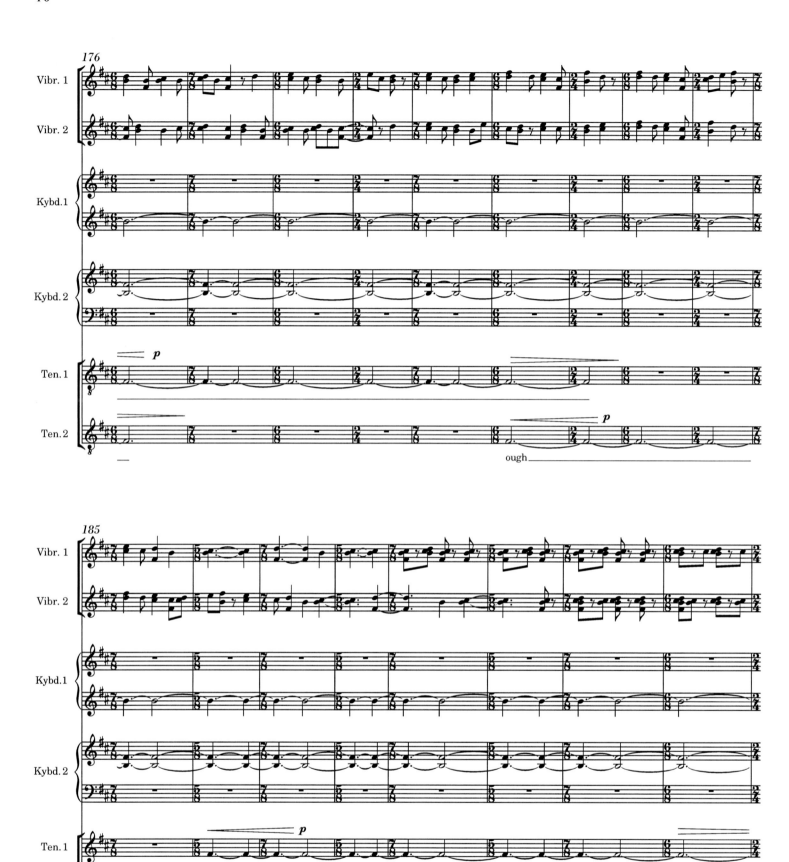

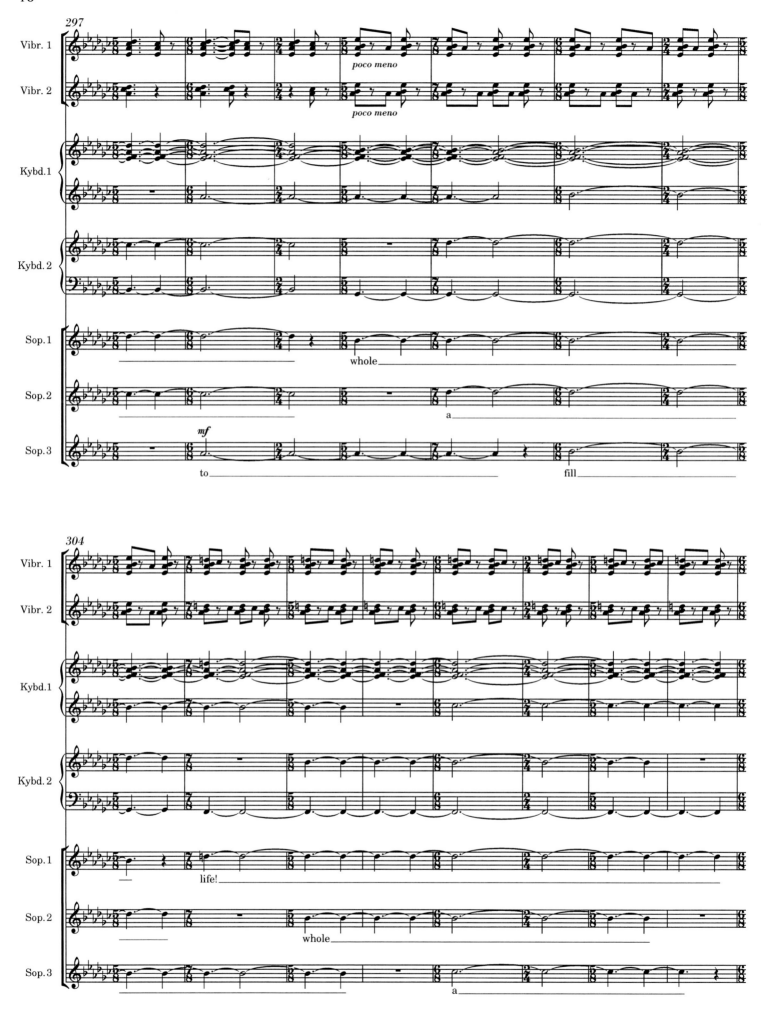

486
Vibr. 1
Vibr. 2
Kybd.1
Kybd. 2
Sop. 1
Sop. 2
Sop. 3
Ten. 1
Ten. 2
mf
a
mf
ill
mf
to
a
a
a
a
a
a
a
a
a
a
497
Vibr. 1
Vibr. 2
Kybd.1
Kybd. 2
Sop. 1
Sop. 2
Sop. 3
Ten. 1
Ten. 2
whole
mf
a
fill
poco meno
ole
ole
ole
ole
ole
poco meno
ole
ole
ole
ole
ole